GOD AMONG US

A Gospel Centered Exploration of
JESUS' MINISTRY

D. A. Horton

LifeWay Press®
Nashville, Tennessee

Item: 005792208
ISBN: 978-1-4300-6550-0
Dewey decimal classification number: 232.95
Subject heading: JESUS CHRIST—TEACHINGS \ JESUS CHRIST—PUBLIC MINISTRY \ DISCIPLESHIP

Eric Geiger
Vice President, LifeWay Resources

Ed Stetzer
General Editor

Trevin Wax
Managing Editor

Michael Kelley
Director, Groups Ministry

Joel Polk
Content Editor

We believe that the Bible has God for its author; salvation for its end; and truth, without any mixture of error, for its matter and that all Scripture is totally true and trustworthy. To review LifeWay's doctrinal guideline, please visit *lifeway.com/doctrinalguideline*.

Unless otherwise noted, all Scripture quotations are taken from the Christian Standard Bible®. Copyright 2017 by Holman Bible Publishers. Used by permission.

For ordering or inquiries, visit *lifeway.com;* write LifeWay Small Groups; One LifeWay Plaza; Nashville, TN 37234-0152; or call toll free (800) 458-2772.

Printed in the United States of America.

Groups Ministry Publishing
LifeWay Resources
One LifeWay Plaza
Nashville, Tennessee 37234-0152

TABLE OF CONTENTS

ABOUT THE GOSPEL PROJECT

Some people see the Bible as a collection of stories with morals for life application. But it's so much more. Sure, the Bible has some stories in it, but it's also full of poetry, history, codes of law and civilization, songs, prophecy, letters—even a love letter. When you tie it all together, something remarkable happens. A story is revealed. One story. The story of redemption through Jesus. This is *The Gospel Project*.

When we begin to see the Bible as the story of redemption through Jesus Christ, God's plan to rescue the world from sin and death, our perspective changes. We no longer look primarily for what the Bible says about us but instead see what it tells us about God and what He has done. After all, it's the gospel that saves us, and when we encounter Jesus in the pages of Scripture, the gospel works on us, transforming us into His image. *We become God's gospel project.*

ABOUT THE WRITER

D.A. HORTON

D.A. Horton currently serves as a pastor at Reach Fellowship, a church plant in Los Angeles, California, and the Chief Evangelist for UYWI. He is also working toward his PhD in Applied Theology at Southeastern Baptist Theological Seminary. He and his wife, Elicia, have three children, Izabelle, Lola, and Damon Jr. (aka Duce).

HOW TO USE THIS STUDY

Welcome to *The Gospel Project*, a gospel-centered small-group study that dives deep into the things of God, lifts up Jesus, focuses on the grand story of Scripture, and drives participants to be on mission. This small-group Bible study provides opportunities to study the Bible and to encounter the living Christ. *The Gospel Project* provides you with tools and resources to purposefully study God's Word and to grow in the faith and knowledge of God's Son. And what's more, you can do so in the company of others, encouraging and building up one another. Here are some things to remember that will help you maximize the usefulness of this resource:

GATHER A GROUP. We grow in the faith best in community with other believers, as we love, encourage, correct, and challenge one another. The life of a disciple of Christ was never meant to be lived alone, in isolation.

PRAY. Pray regularly for your group members.

PREPARE. This resource includes the Bible study content, three devotionals, and discussion questions for each session. Work through the session and devotionals in preparation for each group session. Take notes and record your own questions. Also consider the follow-up questions so you are ready to participate in and add to the discussion, bringing up your own notes and questions where appropriate.

RESOURCE YOURSELF. Make good use of the additional resources available on the Web at *gospelproject.com/additionalresources* and search for this specific title. Download a podcast. Read a blog post. Be intentional about learning from others in the faith. For tips on how to better lead groups or additional ideas for leading this Bible study, visit: *ministrygrid.com/web/thegospelproject*.

GROUP TIME. Gather together with your group to discuss the session and devotional content. Work through the follow-up questions and your own questions. Discuss the material and the implications for the lives of believers and the mission to which we have been called.

OVERFLOW. Remember…*The Gospel Project* is not just a Bible study. *We* are the project. The gospel is working on us. Don't let your preparation time be simply about the content. Let the truths of God's Word soak in as you study. Let God work on your heart first, and then pray that He will change the hearts of the other people in your group.

THE
GOSPEL
PR⊕JECT®

SESSION 1

JESUS CALLS THE FIRST DISCIPLES

"We cannot come thinking we are someone special or a person of privilege. We come with the understanding that we are nothing without Him ... We bow before the Master because godliness demands submission."[1]

TED TRAYLOR

INDIVIDUAL STUDY

Phone calls exist to be answered. In our day, we've gotten good at ignoring them. When our cell phones ring, we usually look at the caller ID to determine whether or not we should answer the call. Sometimes the call comes at a time when we don't want to be interrupted. Other times we decide to return the call later, send a short text, or ignore it altogether.

But there are times we miss a call because our phone is on silent. We pick up our phone to see who reached out to us and then return the call because we hate that we missed the chance to speak with the person. We send a text message or leave a voicemail, apologizing for missing the call earlier and expressing our availability to talk.

In rare cases, we may have to block persistent callers who harass us and won't stop. In the worst cases, we may have to change our phone number.

> **What habits do you have when it comes to making and receiving calls on your phone?**

> **When have those practices been beneficial? When have they been problematic for you?**

Sometimes we treat God's call to repent and follow Jesus the way we treat a caller on the phone. We may choose to ignore God's call, to "silence" it by distancing ourselves from the Scriptures and from other Christians.

In today's session, we see Jesus' call to repentance, a call that He extended to unlikely and unexpected people. Instead of ignoring the call, the first disciples abandoned their old way of life and received Christ's invitation to follow Him. Now, as believers in Christ, we have the privilege of answering God's call to discipleship and then extending the same call to those who need to repent and believe.

Jesus Calls for Repentance

Jesus' methodology of ministry is marked by the use of the phrase "From then on." In Matthew 4:17, this phrase indicates the launch of Jesus' public ministry.

> From then on Jesus began to preach,
> "Repent, because the kingdom of heaven has come near."
> MATTHEW 4:17

Now that Jesus' ministry was public, He called for repentance as the prerequisite for discipleship. To repent means to change one's mind, to turn around in a way that leads to life-change. Jesus was not making a suggestion but issuing a command. The person who hears the command is to make a conscious decision to obey and then live accordingly. To repent means to leave your former way of life to follow Jesus, and repentance is demonstrated through faithfully following Him.

Jesus' ministry started with a command that may have seemed abrupt. But consider how God has been good to His creation by providing us—His creatures—with experiences in life that lead to joy. Our encounters with everyday goodness are not mere coincidences; they are provided by God to soften our hearts toward Him and lead us to repentance. As the apostle Paul said in Romans 2:4: "Do you despise the riches of his kindness, restraint, and patience, not recognizing that God's kindness is intended to lead you to repentance?"

> **Why do you think Matthew summed up Jesus' preaching ministry with this announcement about God's kingdom and the call to repent?**

Jesus' ministry began with the call to repentance, and that leads us to two questions:

WHY DID JESUS CALL FOR REPENTANCE?

Jesus gave a reason the people needed to repent: "Because the kingdom of heaven has come near." That is the announcement that lays the foundation for repentance. Jesus was expressing the truth that God's kingdom—His rule and reign—was coming to earth through Him and His work. God was keeping His promise to bring salvation to sinful humanity and restoration to a broken, fallen world. He was keeping His promise to send the Messiah to make everything right. Because God was acting in this way, Jesus said the people needed to repent to get on board with what God was doing.

So, Jesus' call to repentance is a prerequisite for discipleship. Why? Because being a disciple implies following Jesus as King. You can't follow Jesus as King if you are not repenting of sin and embracing Him as Lord.

WHAT ARE WE TO REPENT OF?

As we read at the beginning of the Bible, Adam and Eve fell into sin. From Adam we inherited a sinful nature (see Rom. 5:12-19) and have become slaves to sin (see John 8:34). When we repent, we admit our need for God's power to save us and our desire to be involved in His kingdom agenda, not our own.

The gospel message proclaims Jesus' perfect life, His death in our place, and His resurrection; and it tells us that Jesus is the only qualified Savior for sinners. We put our faith in Him, and we renounce our sin and our self-righteous attempts to earn salvation. We turn away from our selfishness and sin in order to follow Jesus, the One who brings God's kingdom to earth.

Do you sense urgency in the words of Jesus in this passage? Why or why not?

What is the role of urgency in the call to repentance?

9

2 Jesus Calls the Unlikely

Because Jesus calls everyone to repent, there is no specific "profile" that describes followers of Jesus. The only qualification is repentant faith. Jesus calls people from all backgrounds and every imaginable way of life. Anyone who responds to His call will be saved and assured of a place in the family of God.

If you were picking a team of people to help you change the world, what types of people would you want? Why?

In the next scene, we see Jesus call His first disciples. These first followers were fishermen—probably not the kind of occupation or position in society you'd expect a Messiah to choose from when bringing together men who would change the world. Take a look:

> 18 As he was walking along the Sea of Galilee, he saw two brothers, Simon (who is called Peter), and his brother Andrew. They were casting a net into the sea—for they were fishermen. 19 "Follow me," he told them, "and I will make you fish for people." 20 Immediately they left their nets and followed him.
>
> 21 Going on from there, he saw two other brothers, James the son of Zebedee, and his brother John. They were in a boat with Zebedee their father, preparing their nets, and he called them. 22 Immediately they left the boat and their father and followed him.
> MATTHEW 4:18-22

Jesus didn't choose celebrities with money and influence. He didn't choose politicians with connections or CEOs of Fortune 500 companies with excellent leadership and managerial traits. Instead, He chose two sets of brothers who were all fishermen.

- The first set (Peter and Andrew) were everyday blue-collar workers.

- The second set (James and John) worked for their father, who had hired help (see Mark 1:20), so they may have come from some level of affluence.

In His call, Jesus used a play on words when He took their occupation (fishermen) and turned it around, saying He would make them "fish for people." What's amazing is that both sets of brothers immediately followed Jesus when He called them. They didn't have all the details, they didn't have a destination in mind, but still they obeyed Jesus' call to follow.

Like Abraham, who left his family and country to go to a place promised by God, and like Samuel, who said, "Speak, for your servant is listening" (1 Sam. 3:10), the disciples followed in the footsteps of their faithful ancestors and heeded God's call.

What are some examples from Scripture of men and women who obeyed God when He called them?

What are some examples of people who disobeyed or delayed their obedience?

Today, Jesus is calling people from every walk of life to leave their selfish pursuits and follow Him. It takes wisdom to understand the nature of God's particular call on your life. It may not require that you walk away from your family business or sell all your belongings. But it will definitely require you to give up the idea that you command your own destiny. It will mean you give up any trace of selfish ambition that affects your life decisions. God's kingdom must be first.

As we submit to God, He does amazing things through us. The beauty of God's call to repentance is that He brings together people from various backgrounds and groups in order to highlight His glorious work of redemption. He calls people you'd least expect. He does things you would never predict. He doesn't just call "the cream of the crop" to be His spokespeople but unlikely people whose life-change will demonstrate the glory of His work.

Why is it both comforting and empowering for believers to know and understand that God calls everyday, ordinary people to proclaim His extraordinary gospel?

3 Jesus Calls the Unpopular and Unexpected

Jesus didn't only call fishermen to follow Him; He also called people with despised occupations. Matthew, for example, was a tax-collector.

Jewish tax-collectors had a terrible reputation. They were seen as traitors and swindlers. And yet, Jesus extended His call of discipleship to someone who had this occupation, even when He knew there would be fallout.

> [9] As Jesus went on from there, he saw a man named Matthew sitting at the toll booth, and he said to him, "Follow me," and he got up and followed him.
>
> [10] While he was reclining at the table in the house, many tax collectors and sinners came to eat with Jesus and his disciples. [11] When the Pharisees saw this, they asked his disciples, "Why does your teacher eat with tax collectors and sinners?"
>
> [12] Now when he heard this, he said, "It is not those who are well who need a doctor, but those who are sick. [13] Go and learn what this means: I desire mercy and not sacrifice. For I didn't come to call the righteous, but sinners."
>
> MATTHEW 9:9-13

After Matthew obeyed Jesus and followed Him, he quickly saw his worlds collide. His old world of relationships with tax-collectors and sinners now mixed with his new world of Jesus and the other disciples. Put those two worlds together and, not surprisingly, the tension led to a confrontation. The Pharisees saw who was at the party, and they questioned the faithfulness of Jesus because of the company He was keeping.

Jesus heard their questions, and He answered them by saying the sick are the ones who need a doctor. He didn't come to call the righteous but sinners. It was Jesus' heart to seek and save the lost (see Luke 19:10). Jesus is the great physician seeking to heal those who are spiritually sick, infected by the disease of sin (see Ps. 103:3).

Why do you think the Pharisees felt offended by the people at the dinner?

How should Jesus' response impact the way we think about our own hospitality and ministry?

What kinds of people did Jesus minister to?

As we look at the story of Jesus' earthy ministry, we see a vast array of people He embraced, ministered to, and forgave of their sins.

- He healed an official's son (see John 4:46-54).
- He cleansed the leper (see Matt. 8:2-4).
- He healed the paralytic and forgave his sins (see Matt. 9:1-8).
- He healed the unclean woman with the issue of blood (see Mark 5:25-34).
- He fed the multitudes (see Matt. 15:32-38; John 6:1-14).
- He raised the dead (see Luke 7:11-17; 8:41-56; John 11:1-44).

Jesus sought out all types of people and treated them with dignity by having compassion on them, listening to their pain, and meeting their physical and spiritual needs.

Since we are commanded to imitate Christ (see Eph. 5:1), we have the privilege of taking the gospel to those who are underserved, neglected, and overlooked. The gospel compels us to restore the dignity of society's outcasts by affirming the fact that they, like all humans, were made in the image of God (see Gen. 1:26-27). How will they hear the call of Jesus to repent unless someone who knows Jesus goes to them and shares the gospel, extending the call to repent and the invitation to follow Him?

As followers of Jesus, how can we model His actions to those in need around us?

GROUP STUDY

Warm Up

How do you normally choose the types of people you want as a part of your life?

How do these people compare to the types of people Jesus typically did life with?

"It is … remarkable that Jesus calls Matthew to be his follower, even though society in general and the nation's leadership in particular would have written anyone like him off as beyond saving! Jesus is interested in people regardless of their backgrounds. In part that is why many tax collectors and sinners followed Jesus … Every human being is a sinner and therefore in need of a saviour." [2]

God commands and compels His children to share the good news of the gospel with people everywhere, from all walks of life. We must fight any tendency to profile people and assume they are not redeemable or attractive enough to be ministered to. Don't close your eyes to the world around you. Be aware of the people God has placed in your path. Don't profile people or write off others as beyond the reach of God's grace. Jesus called unlikely people, and He still does.

In what ways might your study this week impact the way you choose who you spend time with in the future?

"From the beginning Jesus took it for granted that people are sinners, and accordingly his first message was that they must repent. Only so would they know the forgiveness he came to bring." [3]

LEON MORRIS

Discussion

1. Why did Jesus call for repentance? What are we to repent of?

2. What is the role of urgency in the call to repentance?

3. If you were picking a team of people to help you change the world, what types of people would you want? Why?

4. What are some examples from Scripture of men and women who obeyed God when He called them?

5. What are some examples of people who disobeyed or delayed their obedience?

6. Why is it both comforting and empowering for believers to know and understand that God calls everyday, ordinary people to proclaim His extraordinary gospel?

7. Why do you think the Pharisees felt offended by the people at the dinner?

8. How should Jesus' response impact the way we think about our own hospitality and ministry?

Conclusion

I once learned a valuable lesson on the streets of Kansas City. My friend and I decided to connect one day to pray for and evangelize the community surrounding our church plant. We noticed a tall, slender man with dirty clothes and a long unkempt beard waving at us. He ran up and told us that the guy who normally sold drugs in that area was not there anymore. We told him we weren't looking for drugs; we were out on the streets sharing the love of God.

During this 30-minute encounter, my friend and I were able to share the gospel with this man. He had been released from prison after receiving a cancer diagnosis. He had just one month to live. That day he prayed to receive Christ.

Later, he told my friend and me that every morning he prayed to God to send him a sign to know if God was pleased with him or not. He said that when he heard the gospel message about his sinfulness, Jesus' work, and the command to repent, his heart was willing to receive God's embrace because he finally knew how he could be in a right relationship with Him.

To be honest, when I first saw that man, I assumed he was homeless and wanted to bum money off us. Sharing the gospel was not my first thought. But now, looking back, I am amazed to think that God put us in that place to share the gospel and call a man to repent—a man who pursued *us*!

Spend some time praying this for you and for your group:

> "God, thank You for calling the unlikely, the unpopular, and the unexpected. Thank You that You call all of us to repentance. Stir in our hearts the desire and willingness to answer Your call to discipleship and extend that same call to those who need to repent and believe, no matter who they are. Amen."

1. Ted Traylor, *The Eight Callings of God* (Bradenton, FL: Outcome Publishing, 2009), 118.
2. Joe Kapolyo, "Matthew," in *Africa Bible Commentary*, ed. Tokunboh Adeyemo (Grand Rapids: Zondervan, 2006) [eBook].
3. Leon Morris, *The Gospel According to Matthew*, in *The Pillar New Testament Commentary* (Grand Rapids: Eerdmans, 2010) [WORDsearch].
4. Kevin DeYoung, "A Friend of Sinners and No Friend of Sin," *The Gospel Coalition* [online], 12 October 2013 [cited 6 July 2016]. Available from the Internet: *thegospelcoalition.org*.

"People reviled Jesus. They called him a glutton and a drunkard, a friend of tax collectors and sinners. Have you ever been called names like this? Have I? Do we fear contamination from the world more than we have confidence in Christ's power to cleanse?" [4]

KEVIN DEYOUNG

NOTES

SESSION 2

NICODEMUS AND THE NEW BIRTH

"Christianity without conversion is no longer Christian,
because conversion means turning to God." [1]

DAVID F. WELLS

INDIVIDUAL STUDY

Toy commercials are usually filled with action. They show kids having fun as they play with whatever product is being promoted. But at the end, a narrator usually comes on and makes a disclaimer: "Batteries not included." I'm sure there have been numerous occasions when well-meaning parents or guardians purchased a toy their child wanted without realizing there were no batteries in the box. The kid feels duped, the parent is embarrassed, and the moment of bliss fades away because the toy can't function.

When have you been disappointed by something not functioning as you thought it would?

What was the reason for the item's inability to function?

As Christians, we believe salvation is a gift. God our Father has shown grace in giving us salvation. But unlike those disappointing toy commercials, this gift doesn't need a disclaimer that says, "Batteries not included." The good news about God's gift is that alongside forgiveness of sins, we receive the Holy Spirit. He is the One who empowers us to live according to God's Word. The spiritual batteries of the Christian life are included because the Holy Spirit takes up residence in us (see Rom. 8:9-13) and gives us strength to walk rightly before God and others.

In this session, we read about Jesus' conversation with Nicodemus. Jesus taught this religious leader about the mystery of regeneration, what He described as being "born again." As Christians, we have been born again by the Spirit of God through faith in God's Son. The new birth is the basis of our confidence that God is at work transforming us and all who believe in the gospel.

New Birth Begins with the Spirit

In John 3, the writer of this Gospel introduces an interesting man who came to see Jesus at night. He was a Pharisee, and his name was Nicodemus.

> [1] There was a man from the Pharisees named Nicodemus, a ruler of the Jews. [2] This man came to him at night and said, "Rabbi, we know that you are a teacher who has come from God, for no one could perform these signs you do unless God were with him."
>
> [3] Jesus replied, "Truly I tell you, unless someone is born again, he cannot see the kingdom of God."
> JOHN 3:1-3

As their conversation began, Nicodemus affirmed Jesus' ministry of teaching and healing. He recognized that Jesus had the blessing of God on His ministry, and so Nicodemus complimented Him for the signs Jesus performed. That's as far as Nicodemus went in attributing any special role to Jesus. It's clear that he saw Jesus as a good teacher, a moral person, and perhaps even a model of how one should live.

Jesus' response was abrupt. He didn't acknowledge the compliments Nicodemus gave. He didn't respond by offering compliments of His own or treating Nicodemus as a peer. Instead, Jesus said no one would see the kingdom of God without being born again. It's impossible to see the salvation of God apart from this experience of being born from above—one can see "signs" but not their significance.

What are some examples of people seeing God at work in the world (signs) but not attributing the work to God or understanding what the work means?

When have you seen God at work and misunderstood His plans?

4 "How can anyone be born when he is old?" Nicodemus asked him. "Can he enter his mother's womb a second time and be born?"

5 Jesus answered, "Truly I tell you, unless someone is born of water and the Spirit, he cannot enter the kingdom of God. 6 Whatever is born of the flesh is flesh, and whatever is born of the Spirit is spirit. 7 Do not be amazed that I told you that you must be born again. 8 The wind blows where it pleases, and you hear its sound, but you don't know where it comes from or where it is going. So it is with everyone born of the Spirit."

9 "How can these things be?" asked Nicodemus.

10 "Are you a teacher of Israel and don't know these things?" Jesus replied.
JOHN 3:4-10

Nicodemus' question was sincere. Because he did not understand what Jesus was teaching, he asked Jesus to clarify. Maybe Nicodemus assumed that since he was a religious leader, he automatically had a right standing with God or already knew God's plan for bringing His kingdom. Maybe he assumed that his religious observance gave him a better position from which to interpret and experience God's mighty works.

Jesus did indeed clarify His initial statement. He revealed to Nicodemus that "new birth" is essential for entering into and experiencing the kingdom of God. One doesn't come into this new relationship with God simply by being spiritual but by yielding to the Holy Spirit. Jesus connected the reality of being "born again" to the necessity of being born of the Spirit. Nicodemus didn't need inside knowledge from Jesus; he needed new birth from the Spirit.

What was missing in the life of Nicodemus?

How does Jesus' interaction with Nicodemus provide a model for how we engage with those who are spiritually minded but not committed to Christ?

2 New Birth Comes Through Faith

The conversation between Nicodemus and Jesus continued, but now Jesus took the lead and began to explain further the "new birth" and its significance. This new and everlasting life comes through faith in Jesus. Take a look:

> [11] "Truly I tell you, we speak what we know and we testify to what we have seen, but you do not accept our testimony. [12] If I have told you about earthly things and you don't believe, how will you believe if I tell you about heavenly things? [13] No one has ascended into heaven except the one who descended from heaven—the Son of Man.
> [14] "Just as Moses lifted up the snake in the wilderness, so the Son of Man must be lifted up, [15] so that everyone who believes in him may have eternal life.
> JOHN 3:11-15

Here, Jesus has forced a dichotomy into the conversation between the religious leaders of Israel and Jesus with His disciples. The religious leaders so far had rejected the testimony of Jesus. This raised an important question: How could the religious leaders compliment Jesus for His teaching on any matter if they had rejected His testimony about Himself?

Jesus didn't wait for an answer. Instead, He claimed to be the One who had descended to earth from heaven. Jesus is the Son of God who took on human flesh in order to reveal the character of God to the world.

What is the connection between a person's identity and the value of his or her testimony?

Next, this conversation took a surprising turn. Jesus reminded Nicodemus of a story in the Old Testament found in Numbers 21:4-9. The Israelites were grumbling about their circumstances. God had brought them out of Egypt, but they failed to obey and take the promised land, so they wandered in the wilderness for 40 years. During this time, God led them, God cared for them, and God provided water and food for them. But they decided they hated the food God gave them in the wilderness. They accused God of having malevolent intentions: "Why have you led us up from Egypt to die in the wilderness?" (v. 5).

The Lord grew angry toward the Israelites and punished them by sending serpents into the camp. The plague of serpents was fierce, and the people began to repent. To save the people from the effects of their sin, God told Moses to put a bronze snake on a pole. Anyone who looked at the snake—who gazed upon that symbol of evil—would be healed.

Jesus compared Himself (the Son of Man) to that snake! He was pointing forward to the moment when He would take upon Himself the weight of our sin, guilt, and shame. The cross would be the symbol of just how evil is our sin as well as the source of our salvation.

In Moses' day, there was no cure apart from God's instruction. The people could have tried their homemade remedies to save themselves from the bites of the serpents, but none of those remedies would have had any effect. There was only one way to be healed, and it was through gazing upon the bronze snake lifted high on the pole. In a similar way, Jesus explained, He, too, would be lifted up. The only way for people to receive eternal life—healing from the sickness of sin and pardon from the penalty of death—would be to gaze upon Him in faith.

Only those who hear the gospel and look to Jesus alone as their sole means of salvation, and believe in His teachings, perfect life, substitutionary death, and resurrection will be born again.

How would you explain the words "faith" and "believe" from a biblical perspective? What similar words would you use?

How does this passage illustrate the meaning of faith?

③ Jesus Is the Gift

We've seen how Jesus instructed Nicodemus concerning eternal life and the need for new birth. Next, we come to one of the most famous verses in the Bible, one that sums up the good news of God's love for the world. Take a moment to consider all we have covered up to this point, and then read the verses after John 3:16 so you can see the verse in context.

> 16 For God loved the world in this way: He gave his one and only Son, so that everyone who believes in him will not perish but have eternal life. 17 For God did not send his Son into the world to condemn the world, but to save the world through him. 18 Anyone who believes in him is not condemned, but anyone who does not believe is already condemned, because he has not believed in the name of the one and only Son of God.
>
> 19 This is the judgment: The light has come into the world, and people loved darkness rather than the light because their deeds were evil. 20 For everyone who does evil hates the light and avoids it, so that his deeds may not be exposed. 21 But anyone who lives by the truth comes to the light, so that his works may be shown to be accomplished by God."
>
> JOHN 3:16-21

The focus here is on how God loved the world, and the love described here is self-sacrificing. Romans 5:8 tells us that God demonstrated His love for us that even while we were still in sin, separated from Him, He sent His Son, Jesus, to seek and save the lost by dying for us. John 3:16 reminds us that God gave His best—Himself in the person of His Son—in the place of sinners like you and me.

It's natural for us to value things that are unique. I remember one time when my wife and I were engaged, she created a Valentine card for me. It was unique, one-of-a-kind, and I still have it in my possession today. It's kept safe because it is significant and meaningful to me.

The card signified the love of my wife for me. But it's the love—not just the card—that matters so much. The good news of God's love for the world is that His love is the foundation of His Son's sacrifice—and this is the love that undergirds our Christian life.

What is the most significant gift you have ever received? What made it meaningful?

In John 3:17, we see that God sent His Son into the world not to judge it but rather to save it. There will come a day when Jesus will judge the non-believing world, and all who reject God's free gift of salvation through Christ will receive the consequences. But before judgment comes we receive the extending of grace. Before judgment comes we receive the appeal of God's Son to all humanity.

John wrote that those who reject Jesus already stand condemned before God. The good news is that Christ came to be executed in our place. By grace through faith, we can be set free from the prison of sin and given a new life in Christ because the sentence has been carried out.

Unfortunately, as this passage shows us, humans naturally love darkness (the sinful deeds and lifestyle we're born into) rather than the light of Jesus Christ. We live in a society where people entertain the false understanding that one can have Jesus plus their sin; to have Jesus as their light even while they pursue the deeds of darkness.

But this passage shows us the reality of what life looks like for those who have embraced Jesus: "But anyone who lives by the truth comes to the light, so that his works may be shown to be accomplished by God" (John 3:21). Those who come to Jesus want His light to expose all of their life so that He can continue His work of renovating us from the inside out.

Imagine your heart as a spiritual home, and when you embrace God's gift of salvation through Jesus, He becomes the owner of the house, as God the Holy Spirit takes up residence inside of you. As the homeowner, God has the right to go through every room and make the renovations He desires because He owns the home.

Sometimes I wonder if we feel more comfortable being a tour guide for Jesus walking through our home—as if we can keep certain rooms off-limits to Him. Jesus is the light. He shines into every nook and cranny of our hearts and brings about His transforming power.

In what areas of your life does it feel uncomfortable for the light of Christ to shine?

How does God's gift of salvation impact these areas of your life?

GROUP STUDY

Warm Up

What is the most significant gift you have ever received? What made it meaningful?

What is the most significant gift you have ever given? What made it significant to you?

A person gives a gift to someone he or she feels is important. The gift-giver has likely spent time and effort choosing exactly the right gift. We don't give a gift just to go through the motions. We want the receiver to feel special, valued, loved, known. Isn't that a good feeling? And how much more so when the gift comes from the Lord Himself?

God has provided for us a free gift—salvation through Christ. The preciousness of this gift is appreciated at a greater level of understanding when we recognize the unique nature of Jesus. He is referred to as the one and only, the "only begotten," which means He is unique and can never be replicated.

How can you live your days as a good steward of this precious gift?

"Oh, what a gift of grace this is that is freely given to us by God! 'God so loved the world that He gave His only begotten Son' (John 3:16). He is God's unspeakable gift." [2]

CHARLES SPURGEON

Discussion

1. What are some examples of people seeing God at work in the world (signs) but not attributing the work to God or understanding what the work means?

2. When have you seen God at work and misunderstood His plans?

3. What was missing in the life of Nicodemus?

4. How does Jesus' interaction with Nicodemus provide a model for how we engage with those who are spiritually minded but not committed to Christ?

5. What is the connection between a person's identity and the value of his or her testimony?

6. How would you explain the words "faith" and "believe" from a biblical perspective? What similar words would you use?

7. In what areas of your life does it feel uncomfortable for the light of Christ to shine?

8. How does God's gift of salvation impact these areas of your life?

Conclusion

The work of regeneration is a supernatural work of God, not the natural work of man. Nevertheless, the responsibility of getting the message of the gospel out is the work God has called every believer to participate in. We should never assume that because people are familiar with religion, Christianity, or even the church that they know Jesus as their Savior. God has called every believer to trust in His power as we are transformed by the Holy Spirit.

Nicodemus was a religious man who was interested in Jesus' teaching. Jesus told Nicodemus that he needed new life, not more religious activities. Jesus' teaching on the new birth reminds us that there is no spiritual life apart from Jesus. God loved the world in this way: He gave His Son so that everyone who believes in Him will not perish but have eternal life.

Spend some time praying this for you and for your group:

> "God, we come before You with humble and grateful hearts. Thank You that Jesus has already taken the execution sentence in our place and that by grace through faith, we are assured of a new life in Christ. Teach us to trust in Your transformational power in our lives. Amen."

1. David F. Wells, quoted in *New Dictionary of Christian Ethics & Pastoral Theology*, eds. David J. Atkinson and David F. Field (Downers Grove: IVP, 1995), 288.
2. Charles Spurgeon, in *The Essential Works of Charles Spurgeon*, ed. Daniel Partner (Uhrichsville, OH: Barbour, 2009) [eBook].
3. Lesslie Newbigin, *The Light Has Come: An Exposition of the Fourth Gospel* (Grand Rapids: Eerdmans, 1982), 42.

"To 'enter into the kingship of God' can only be by the gift of a new life, the life of God himself, and that gift can only be made available by the descent of God himself to pour out his life in death for the life of the world." [3]

LESSLIE NEWBIGIN

NOTES

SESSION 3

JESUS AND JOHN THE BAPTIST

"Jesus is being held up as glorious—magnificent, splendid, supreme—full of grace and truth. And as we are enabled to see him for who he really is, grace upon grace streams into our lives. And Jesus becomes for us the most precious reality in the world—forgiving all our sins, providing all our righteousness, and becoming an all-satisfying Treasure and Friend." [1]

JOHN PIPER

INDIVIDUAL STUDY

A few years ago, I was with my daughter at an event where we received some "glow sticks," something I had to explain to my daughter, who was only four years old at the time. My daughter was unhappy with her glow stick because it wasn't glowing, so she told me to throw it away. I said, "Of course it's not working. It's not broken yet. It won't work until it's broken." She was puzzled but intrigued. I took her glow stick, snapped it in half, and immediately the fluorescent orange appeared out of nowhere. Her eyes opened wide and she squealed, "Daddy, do it again!" I continued to break the glow stick in various places until it was totally consumed with the glow.

I think back to that occasion whenever I read about God using broken people to further His purposes. Brokenness—the bending of our will and the humbling of our hearts—is a prerequisite to being used by God. Whenever we ask God to rid us of our pride and to break our wills, we are asking Him to do something that will allow us to shine for His glory. We won't glow with love for God until we're broken and humbled by God's love for us.

> **Why is it necessary to be broken and humbled for God to work through us?**

> **In what ways does humility help us follow Jesus faithfully?**

In this session, we will see how John the Baptist prepared the way for Jesus by pointing to Him and His kingdom, by finding his greatest joy in Jesus' exaltation, and by warning others and witnessing to the love and power of God. Because John recognized his purpose and his identity, he offered his heart with joyful gladness to the Messiah who was coming. From John we learn how to find our identity in Christ and how our mission goes forward as people who "decrease" in order that Christ may receive all the glory.

1 John's Mission—Pointing to the Messiah

At this point in the Gospel storyline, the vibrant ministry of John the Baptist is beginning to wane and the ministry of Jesus is just getting started. During this period of transition from John the Baptist to Jesus, there could have been major disputes, a falling out, or some sort of conflict between Jesus and John. Instead, John the Baptist handled his declining popularity and Jesus' rise with the kind of humility and confidence that is characteristic of someone who knew his mission.

> ²² After this, Jesus and his disciples went to the Judean countryside, where he spent time with them and baptized.
> ²³ John also was baptizing in Aenon near Salim, because there was plenty of water there. People were coming and being baptized,
> ²⁴ since John had not yet been thrown into prison.
>
> ²⁵ Then a dispute arose between John's disciples and a Jew about purification.
> ²⁶ So they came to John and told him, "Rabbi, the one you testified about, and who was with you across the Jordan, is baptizing—and everyone is going to him."
>
> ²⁷ John responded, "No one can receive anything unless it has been given to him from heaven. ²⁸ You yourselves can testify that I said, 'I am not the Messiah, but I've been sent ahead of him.'"
> JOHN 3:22-28

Some of John's followers, his disciples, came up to him with a problem on their minds. They were concerned about matters related to ceremonial washing and ritual purification. They were also curious about the rise of Jesus' ministry and why His disciples were performing baptisms, just as John was doing. Perhaps the disciples of John felt like Jesus' rising popularity was a threat to their own work. Whatever their motivations, they came to John with questions.

When have you felt like the success of someone else was a threat to you personally or a signal that you were inadequate? How did you respond?

How do you think John's disciples expected him to respond to their questions?

John the Baptist's response was seasoned with humility. He attributed the growth of Jesus' ministry to God, not gimmicks, bells, whistles, or first-century Jewish marketing schemes.

On a deeper level, John recognized that Jesus' ministry was always designed to supplant his own. That's why John reminded his followers that he was not the Messiah and that the Messiah's work would be greater than his. What's remarkable in this response is how content John seems to be with these developments. He could be humble and confident because John knew what his role was—to point people to the Messiah!

Like John, we are called to point people to Jesus and away from ourselves. However, fulfilling our mission of pointing others to Christ is impossible unless we intentionally leverage the gifts God has given us for His glory, not as a distraction that brings attention to ourselves. Our mission is to point people to Jesus. We should do everything we can not to get in the way!

Whenever our pride leads us to begin to seek glory for ourselves, we fall into the trap of making ourselves more and more attractive in order to gain more and more followers. Then, instead of celebrating Jesus, we begin to compete with each other. Our zeal is no longer for the gospel and for God's glory but for the building of our own kingdom. John the Baptist's ministry challenges us to find our ultimate purpose in bringing glory to Christ.

In what ways does your mission today resemble that of John the Baptist's?

2 John's Manner—Humble & Joyful

As John the Baptist's response to his disciples continued, we catch a glimpse of his character—his inner joy at the coming of the Messiah. Don't miss the connection here between John's humility ("I must decrease") and John's joy ("this joy of mine is complete").

> 29 "He who has the bride is the groom. But the groom's friend, who stands by and listens for him, rejoices greatly at the groom's voice. So this joy of mine is complete. 30 He must increase, but I must decrease."
>
> JOHN 3:29-30

As John the Baptist explained his reasons for being joyful, not envious, of Jesus' ministry, he turned to a common illustration of a wedding. John's analogy went like this: "I am like the best man at a wedding feast, and Jesus is like the groom. As the groom's friend, I find great joy in the groom marrying his bride."

Like other friends of the groom, John was saying that his role was to prepare things for the wedding, to assist the groom whenever possible, and to serve the groom well. At a wedding, it is the groom's day to be in the spotlight, not the groomsmen.

When have you found great joy in helping someone who was in the spotlight or center of attention?

What was that experience like?

John the Baptist's analogy of the wedding feast reminds me of a time I served as a groomsman for a close friend of mine. On the day of his wedding, a number of issues arose that were stressing out the couple before the ceremony—quirky things that kept them from savoring their special day.

An hour before the ceremony, I noticed the groom was sitting down with his face in the palm of his hands. Several of us walked over to him and asked him what was wrong. The ushers had not shown, the caterer was late, and family members were fussing about where they were sitting.

The other groomsmen and I sprang into action. We divvied up the different responsibilities and put out all of the "small fires" within 30 minutes. The wedding went on without a hitch. Later that evening, right before he left on his honeymoon, the groom was bursting with gratitude for all we had done. I remember how joyful I felt in knowing we had served the groom well.

> "It is here that John's greatness is supremely brought to our notice; that when he could be thought to be the Christ, he preferred to bear witness to the Christ, to bring him to our notice ... He preferred to humble himself rather than to be taken for the Christ and taken in by himself."[2]
>
> AUGUSTINE

John the Baptist found complete joy in his subservient role to Jesus. He recognized Jesus was the groom, the center of attention, the long-awaited Messiah. John understood that his role was to make sure that the Groom would be exalted and that no distractions would hinder Jesus.

John the Baptist's words here give us a model for how we should find our joy. It should be our goal, drive, and practice to see Jesus lifted up and exalted above everyone and everything. Our joy should come from the fact that Jesus is being made known more widely and deeply. When God breaks us of the callous pride we have in our hearts, we are then able to find joy in humility—in a humble posture that seeks to make much of Jesus and to make ourselves of no reputation.

What areas of your life make it hard for you to find "complete joy" in Jesus?

What is the relation of pride or humility to those areas of your life?

3 John's Message—Warning & Witness

Next we dig into John the Baptist's relation to Jesus. As the passage continues, we see how John the Baptist was a witness to Jesus—a witness who testified that Jesus was sent by God and a witness who warned that rejecting Jesus was rejecting eternal life. Take a look:

> 31 The one who comes from above is above all. The one who is from the earth is earthly and speaks in earthly terms. The one who comes from heaven is above all. 32 He testifies to what he has seen and heard, and yet no one accepts his testimony. 33 The one who has accepted his testimony has affirmed that God is true. 34 For the one whom God sent speaks God's words, since he gives the Spirit without measure. 35 The Father loves the Son and has given all things into his hands. 36 The one who believes in the Son has eternal life, but the one who rejects the Son will not see life; instead, the wrath of God remains on him.
>
> JOHN 3:31-36

John the Baptist saw Jesus as superior, both in where Jesus came from and also in what He taught. John's witness to Christ focused first on Jesus' origin. Jesus is the Messiah who comes from heaven, while John was a witness who was from the earth. The point here is that John the Baptist was under the authority of Jesus because Jesus came from heaven.

Next, see how this passage shows that Jesus' teaching is superior to John the Baptist's. Everything Jesus taught was and is true. Everything Jesus said about Himself being the Messiah, the promised One, was and is true. The point here is that John was a witness to Jesus, while Jesus spoke the very words of God. Not only that, but Jesus also had the power to give the Spirit to those who believe and accept His testimony.

These passages are a great summary of how John the Baptist pointed to Jesus' supremacy:

- Jesus is from heaven, while John was from the earth.

- Jesus speaks the words of God, while John spoke about Jesus.

- Jesus gives the Spirit and life, while John affirmed Jesus' testimony.

What truths about Jesus should be part of our sharing the gospel?

What do these truths communicate about Jesus?

John the Baptist not only witnessed to others about Jesus' identity; he also warned people of the consequences of rejecting Jesus. It is here that John brought up the wrath of God as the opposite of eternal life. Those who do not believe in Jesus or accept Jesus' testimony about Himself are under the wrath of God—God's good and righteous judgment against sin. Whether they realize it or not, those who do not believe are on the road to destruction.

In reading John the Baptist's warning against rejecting the Son, I'm reminded of the sobering reality that God already knows all of our sin. He is gracious and patient, offering us the gift of eternal life and calling us away from a life of sin and death.

But God is also truthful when He declares that the day will come when those who persist in sin will face His just judgment. John the Baptist's witness was not merely about the glory of Christ; it was also about being saved from the wrath of God. Because of Jesus' sacrifices, we are saved from the punishment our sin deserves. Faithful witnessing to the love of God means we call people to be saved from God's wrath.

What role does speaking of God's judgment have in our witness to Jesus?

What happens when we minimize or neglect this part of our message?

Warm Up

The Gospels teach us about one of the greatest men who ever lived, but this man was so humble that he knew he paled in comparison to the Man he was called to point to. John the Baptist was the forerunner to the Messiah, and in humility, he ran in his lane well. He decreased so that the reputation and ministry of Jesus could increase. That's humility. And in John we see what it looks like to make less of ourselves so we can make more of Jesus.

Are there attitudes and motivations getting in the way of you decreasing and instead increasing your focus on Jesus and His mission? Explain.

John the Baptist said he wasn't the bridegroom but the friend of the bridegroom. As the friend, it was his responsibility to decrease in stature and take joy in the groom's wedding. Jesus is the Bridegroom from above who came to give His life for His bride—those who receive His Word and believe in Him. God calls us to find joy in pointing others not to ourselves or to our accomplishments but to the soul-satisfying, self-giving Savior.

What are some ways we can point to the Messiah in our homes? At work? In our community?

"Lost people are more amazed at our silence than offended at our message."[3]

ALVIN REID

Discussion

1. When have you felt like the success of someone else was a threat to you personally or a signal that you were inadequate? How did you respond?

2. How do you think John's disciples expected him to respond to their questions?

3. In what ways does our mission today resemble that of John the Baptist's?

4. What areas of your life make it hard for you to find "complete joy" in Jesus?

5. What is the relation of pride or humility to those areas of your life?

6. What truths about Jesus should be part of our sharing the gospel? What do these truths communicate about Jesus?

7. What role does speaking of God's judgment have in our witness to Jesus?

8. What happens when we minimize or neglect this part of our message?

Conclusion

John the Baptist was a firsthand witness of the ministry of Jesus. Because of John's humility, he was able to take joy in the fact that Jesus was becoming known, even more known than John was at the time. John coupled his joyful expression with a timely warning that it was not enough just to acknowledge Jesus or to crowd around Him while He was ministering. Rather, what God wanted was for the people to listen to the testimony of Jesus and embrace Him as their Lord and Savior.

Nothing should bring more joy and satisfaction to our hearts than seeing people know and embrace Jesus as their Savior. We must take on the humble posture of John the Baptist and see ourselves as a friend to the Groom, pointing away from ourselves and to Jesus Christ—the one and only. We shine the spotlight on Him, not ourselves.

Spend some time praying this for you and for your group:

"God, teach us how to humble our hearts toward You. Thank You that our brokenness in Your hands can be used to humble us so we can glow for Your glory in the darkness of this world. The goal, then, is to turn the attention and the affection of people toward You as we make You known."

1. John Piper, "The Father Has Given All Things into Jesus' Hands," *Desiring God* [online], 31 May 2009 [cited 11 July 2016]. Available from the Internet: *www.desiringgod.org.*
2. Augustine, Sermon, 288.2, quoted in John 1–10, ed. Joel C. Elowsky, vol. IVa in *Ancient Christian Commentary on Scripture: New Testament,* (Downers Grove: IVP, 2006), 134.
3. Alvin Reid, "Practical Evangelism," *The Gospel Project: Adult Leader Guide* (Spring 2015): 142.
4. Christopher J. H. Wright, *The Mission of God* (Downers Grove: IVP, 2006), 66-67.

"When you know who God is, when you know who Jesus is, witnessing mission is the unavoidable outcome."[4]

CHRISTOPHER WRIGHT

NOTES

SESSION 4

JESUS AND THE SAMARITAN WOMAN

"The worshiping heart does not create its Object. It finds Him here when it wakes from its moral slumber in the morning of its regeneration." [1]

A.W. TOZER

INDIVIDUAL STUDY

The good news of the gospel is that God can save anyone, and He does. He saves people from different backgrounds, different ethnicities, and different lifestyles.

I love seeing God work in the hearts of people who are economically well off and those who are disadvantaged. I love seeing Him change the hearts of people you'd least expect. After all, that's what God did for me. While I was running away from God, His grace chased me down. Jesus' followers shared the gospel with me, and the Holy Spirit used their words to stir within me a desire to worship God in Spirit and in truth.

In previous sessions, we saw how Jesus interacted with Nicodemus—a religious man who came to visit Jesus at night. We saw how Jesus' ministry intersected with and then transcended the ministry of John the Baptist. Now the apostle John shows us another scene of Jesus' interaction. This time Jesus speaks with a woman whose ethnicity and past would have made her seem "beyond the reach" of God's grace.

When you think of people who seem "beyond the reach" of God's grace, what characteristics come to mind?

How do accounts of Jesus showing grace to all kinds of people challenge these stereotypes?

In this session, we listen in on a conversation between Jesus and a Samaritan woman He met at the well of Jacob. In their discussion, Jesus claimed to have the living water that will satisfy the soul, and He revealed the truth that God seeks people to worship Him in Spirit and truth. As Jesus' followers, we resemble the Samaritan woman as we exalt Jesus for who He is and then tell others about the living water He offers.

1 Jesus Gives Living Water

The story of Jesus' interaction with the woman at the well begins with a couple of geographical details essential to understanding the dynamics of the conversation about to take place.

> [1] When Jesus learned that the Pharisees had heard he was making and baptizing more disciples than John [2] (though Jesus himself was not baptizing, but his disciples were), [3] he left Judea and went again to Galilee. [4] He had to travel through Samaria; [5] so he came to a town of Samaria called Sychar near the property that Jacob had given his son Joseph. [6] Jacob's well was there, and Jesus, worn out from his journey, sat down at the well. It was about noon.
>
> JOHN 4:1-6

Jesus rejected the culturally acceptable route for Jews that went around the Samaritans. Instead, He took the direct route, and this decision put Him at Jacob's well around noontime, when the social outcasts came to draw water.

How does the gospel speak to the forms of segregation our society has created?

What do we learn from Jesus' model of breaking down cultural barriers in His search for the lost?

> [7] A woman of Samaria came to draw water.
>
> "Give me a drink," Jesus said to her, [8] because his disciples had gone into town to buy food.
>
> [9] "How is it that you, a Jew, ask for a drink from me, a Samaritan woman?" she asked him. For Jews do not associate with Samaritans.
>
> [10] Jesus answered, "If you knew the gift of God, and who is saying to you, 'Give me a drink,' you would ask him, and he would give you living water."

¹¹ "Sir," said the woman, "you don't even have a bucket, and
the well is deep. So where do you get this 'living water'? ¹² You
aren't greater than our father Jacob, are you? He gave us the well
and drank from it himself, as did his sons and livestock."

¹³ Jesus said, "Everyone who drinks from this water will get thirsty
again. ¹⁴ But whoever drinks from the water that I will give him
will never get thirsty again. In fact, the water I will give him will
become a well of water springing up in him for eternal life."

¹⁵ "Sir," the woman said to him, "give me this water so that
I won't get thirsty and come here to draw water."
JOHN 4:7-15

Here we read the dialogue between Jesus and a woman who was likely considered a social
outcast. In Jesus' day, such a conversation was taboo. A teacher of the law or a rabbi would
avoid talking to a woman, especially one from this ethnic background and with her social
history, which we will see in the next section.

"Don't you realize I'm a Samaritan?" The woman saw herself as "out of bounds" and "cast out"
by the Jews and perhaps devalued because of her ethnicity.

But Jesus advanced the conversation in a way that implied this conversation was God's gift to
her. He steered their discussion to the need for living water—the gift of salvation, the gift of
God Himself through the work of Jesus the Son and the indwelling of the Holy Spirit.

What are some examples of "earthly" water that people drink from in
order to quench their spiritual thirst?

How do we know that these other sources of water do not satisfy?

2 Jesus Makes True Worship Possible

As the conversation between Jesus and the Samaritan woman continues, we see a shift toward the woman's personal situation. Take a look:

16 "Go call your husband," he told her, "and come back here."

17 "I don't have a husband," she answered.

"You have correctly said, 'I don't have a husband,'" Jesus said. 18 "For you've had five husbands, and the man you now have is not your husband. What you have said is true."

19 "Sir," the woman replied, "I see that you are a prophet. 20 Our fathers worshiped on this mountain, but you Jews say that the place to worship is in Jerusalem."

21 Jesus told her, "Believe me, woman, an hour is coming when you will worship the Father neither on this mountain nor in Jerusalem. 22 You Samaritans worship what you do not know. We worship what we do know, because salvation is from the Jews. 23 But an hour is coming, and is now here, when the true worshipers will worship the Father in Spirit and in truth. Yes, the Father wants such people to worship him. 24 God is spirit, and those who worship him must worship in Spirit and in truth."

JOHN 4:16-24

It is interesting to note how Jesus took the conversation in a personal direction after having engaged this woman on friendly terms. The discussion about water prompted Jesus to speak the truth about spiritual thirst that only God can quench. Then the discussion about the woman's marital history led to a demonstration of Jesus' ability to know the hearts of people. "You are a prophet," the woman said in response, and she was right.

Even when the woman tried to redirect the topic away from her marital history and toward the location of worship, Jesus kept the focus on her heart. He claimed that God was seeking worshipers in Spirit and in truth. Don't miss what Jesus was implying—this woman was one of the people God was seeking.

What are some ways we sidestep certain subjects in order to avoid talking about the state of our relationship with God?

Jesus informed the Samaritan woman that worship would no longer be bound by geographic location. God was calling people everywhere to pursue Him, to worship Him rightly. The doors of salvation were opening wide to the whole world.

The key, however, is that God desired people to worship Him rightly. To worship in Spirit and truth means we must be born again in order to give acceptable worship to God. He alone is the One who can lead us to worship in Spirit and truth. This worship must be saturated in the Scriptures and must focus our attention on Jesus.

As Kevin Vanhoozer writes: "Right worship proceeds from right knowledge of God … Focusing on the right object is everything in worship. Ignorant worship fails to invigorate or to quench our spiritual thirst. Ignorant worship is a liturgy of death, not life. In Jeremiah God says: 'My people have committed two sins: they have forsaken me, the spring of living water, and have dug their own cisterns, broken cisterns that cannot hold water' (Jer. 2:13). Through our own efforts we can attain neither a right knowledge nor a right worship of God." [2]

What are the characteristics of worshiping in Spirit and in truth?

Can worship be in Spirit but not in truth? In truth but not in Spirit? Why or why not?

3 Jesus Sends Us on Mission

We've seen in this conversation that Jesus offers living water that satisfies spiritual thirst forever. We've also seen that Jesus is the Prophet who reveals the truth that the Father is seeking worshipers in Spirit and truth. Now we see the response of the disciples when they noticed Jesus was talking with this woman. We also see the woman's response to this conversation.

[25] The woman said to him, "I know that the Messiah is coming" (who is called Christ). "When he comes, he will explain everything to us."

[26] Jesus told her, "I, the one speaking to you, am he."

[27] Just then his disciples arrived, and they were amazed that he was talking with a woman. Yet no one said, "What do you want?" or "Why are you talking with her?"

[28] Then the woman left her water jar, went into town, and told the people, [29] "Come, see a man who told me everything I ever did. Could this be the Messiah?" [30] They left the town and made their way to him.

[31] In the meantime the disciples kept urging him, "Rabbi, eat something."

[32] But he said, "I have food to eat that you don't know about."

[33] The disciples said to one another, "Could someone have brought him something to eat?"

[34] "My food is to do the will of him who sent me and to finish his work," Jesus told them. [35] "Don't you say, 'There are still four more months, and then comes the harvest'? Listen to what I'm telling you: Open your eyes and look at the fields, because they are ready for harvest. [36] The reaper is already receiving pay and gathering fruit for eternal life, so that the sower and reaper can rejoice together. [37] For in this case the saying is true: 'One sows and another reaps.' [38] I sent you to reap what you didn't labor for; others have labored, and you have benefited from their labor."

39 Now many Samaritans from that town believed in him because of what the woman said when she testified, "He told me everything I ever did." 40 So when the Samaritans came to him, they asked him to stay with them, and he stayed there two days. 41 Many more believed because of what he said. 42 And they told the woman, "We no longer believe because of what you said, since we have heard for ourselves and know that this really is the Savior of the world."
JOHN 4:25-42

This passage is all about mission. First, the woman made a comment about the Messiah coming to make things right. It was an attempt to put off any decision or claim that Jesus as a prophet might make on her. But Jesus instantly revealed to her that He was the Messiah she was speaking about.

That's when the plot thickens. The disciples who had gone into town to find food arrived at this pivotal moment of Jesus' conversation with the Samaritan woman. They wondered about His motives for breaking cultural protocol, for ignoring ethical and cultural barriers. While they were questioning in their hearts what Jesus was doing, the Samaritan woman left her jar of earthly water and ran back into town. As soon as she understood that Jesus was the Messiah, she dropped everything and told others about Him. She had just met Jesus and was ready for everyone else to meet Him, too.

Has there been a season in your walk with Christ when you were more sharing of the gospel than in your current season? What made the difference?

Through the ministry of the Samaritan woman, God brought many in that city to trust in Jesus. They were made curious by the words of the woman, but when they encountered Jesus the Messiah, they believed for themselves. This is the model for evangelism.

How was the message of Jesus sown in your life, drawing you to faith in Him?

Warm Up

Some of the greatest and most passionate evangelists are people who have recently embraced Jesus. They are filled with excitement to tell others about the good news of what God has done. Unfortunately, it's easy to lose that initial awe and wonder at God's salvation. And with that loss of passion, we share the gospel less and less.

> Why is it easy for us to lose our passion for sharing the good news of Jesus with the lost?

> What can we do about it?

As the Samaritan woman was running through town telling people about the Messiah, the disciples urged Jesus to eat, but Jesus told them He found satisfaction in doing the will of God. Jesus was hungry, but His purpose in this conversation was to emphasize the joy of ministry and how the sacrifice of doing God's will outweighs all other concerns. Serving people the food of God's Word is more important than any other kind of feast.

> How can you be a part of serving people the food of God's Word in your present life circumstances, specifically across cultural barriers?

"The gospel comes to us in order that it might run through us."[3]

SCOTTY SMITH

Discussion

1. How does the gospel speak to the forms of segregation our society has created?

2. What do we learn from Jesus' model of breaking down cultural barriers in His search for the lost?

3. What are some examples of "earthly" water that people drink from in order to quench their spiritual thirst?

4. How do we know that these other sources of water do not satisfy?

5. What are some ways we sidestep certain subjects in order to avoid talking about the state of our relationship with God?

6. What are the characteristics of worshiping in Spirit and in truth?

7. Can worship be in Spirit but not in truth? In truth but not in Spirit? Why or why not?

8. Has there been a season in your walk with Christ when you were more sharing of the gospel than in your current season? What made the difference?

Conclusion

As we saw in the previous sessions, when God the Holy Spirit begins to do the supernatural work that only He can do, regeneration takes place. Through faith, sinners are born again and made saints and are now able to worship God in Spirit and in truth. God has privileged us with the call to go and make our Messiah known because He is looking for worshipers.

Through the ministry of Jesus, worshiping God is no longer bound by geographic location, gender, or ethnicity. Galatians 3:26-28 makes us aware that salvation is open and available for sinners from every imaginable background. Like Jesus told the disciples, the harvest of people in our vicinity is great. We need God to open our eyes to see people around us and to open our mouths to speak His truth and lead them to Christ. And like the Samaritan woman, we say, "Come and see!"

Spend some time praying this for you and for your group:

> "God, we worship You in Spirit and truth. As Your followers, help us resemble the Samaritan woman as we exalt You for who You are and then tell others about the living water You offer. Rekindle our hearts and refresh us with a desire to share Your love with the world."

1. A. W. Tozer, in *Tozer on Worship and Entertainment*, comp. James L. Snyder (Camp Hill, PA: Wing Spread Publishers, 2006) [eBook].
2. Kevin J. Vanhoozer, *Pictures at a Theological Exhibition* (Downers Grove: IVP, 2016), 114-15.
3. Scotty Smith in *Gospel Transformation Bible* (Wheaton: Crossway, 2013), 1414, n. 4:27-38; n. 4:39-43.
4. Caesarius of Arles, Sermon, 170.4, quoted in John 1–10, ed. Joel C. Elowsky, vol. IVa in *Ancient Christian Commentary on Scripture: New Testament*, 150-51.

"Our Lord, the living fountain, came to cleanse the hearts of all people, to quench their thirst and to satisfy their souls." [4]

CAESARIUS OF ARLES

NOTES

SESSION 5

JESUS REJECTED IN NAZARETH

"The portrait of Jesus in this section is of someone who is empowered by the Holy Spirit. This empowering divides those Jesus meets into two groups: those who recognize God in Jesus' words and works and those who do not." [1]

PAUL JOHN ISAAK

INDIVIDUAL STUDY

I love stories about people who overcame seasons of failure or moments of rejection before they discovered success—stories about R. H. Macy, Walt Disney, and Albert Einstein, to name a few. As much as these stories inspire me, I gravitate toward stories of Christians overcoming various forms of opposition through the ministry of the Spirit, who makes known the glory of Jesus through their sufferings. There is nothing like hearing stories of believers whose faith shines bright during times of adversity.

I recently met a man whose family came from a different religious heritage. When his parents converted to Christianity, he was enraged. He rejected his parents and joined the rest of his family in antagonizing them for their newfound faith. But over time, God broke through the hardness of this man's heart, and the man put his faith in Jesus. In our conversations together, we discussed the reconciliation process he would undergo with his parents, but we also recognized the adversity he would face from the other members of the family. I've been blessed to watch this man demonstrate courage and confidence in facing rejection.

Courage and confidence. Those two characteristics are available to every believer through the power of the Holy Spirit. And those two characteristics are visible in the life of Jesus when He faced rejection from the people who knew Him best.

When have you felt rejected by someone?

How does the closeness of your relationship to someone influence the feeling of rejection?

In this session, we see Jesus speaking in the synagogue in His hometown of Nazareth. After He read the words of Scripture, Jesus claimed to be the fulfillment of Isaiah's prophecy and that His mission was to free people held by various types of bondage and sin. The people in Jesus' town rejected Him as a prophet and rejected His message of liberation. As followers of Jesus, we should expect to face opposition and experience hostility because of the gospel, but we can also depend on the Holy Spirit's power to endure.

1 Jesus Declared He Was the Messiah

Luke 4:14-15 places the ministry of Jesus in the region of Galilee. Through His teaching and miracles, Jesus demonstrated the power of the Holy Spirit. The news about His ministry spread, and people began to praise Him for the good work He was doing. But now the scene shifts, and Luke wants us to see the contrast between Jesus' reception in Galilee and His rejection in Nazareth, the place where He grew up.

> [14] Then Jesus returned to Galilee in the power of the Spirit, and news about him spread throughout the entire vicinity. [15] He was teaching in their synagogues, being praised by everyone.
>
> [16] He came to Nazareth, where he had been brought up. As usual, he entered the synagogue on the Sabbath day and stood up to read. [17] The scroll of the prophet Isaiah was given to him, and unrolling the scroll, he found the place where it was written:
>
> [18] The Spirit of the Lord is on me,
>   because he has anointed me
>   to preach good news to the poor.
>   He has sent me
>   to proclaim release to the captives
>   and recovery of sight to the blind,
>   to set free the oppressed,
> [19] to proclaim the year of the Lord's favor.
>
> [20] He then rolled up the scroll, gave it back to the attendant, and sat down. And the eyes of everyone in the synagogue were fixed on him. [21] He began by saying to them, "Today as you listen, this Scripture has been fulfilled." [22] They were all speaking well of him and were amazed by the gracious words that came from his mouth; yet they said, "Isn't this Joseph's son?"
>
> LUKE 4:14-22

When Jesus went into the synagogue, as was the custom, He stood up to read a passage of Scripture. The reading for that day was part of a prophecy from Isaiah that spoke of the coming Messiah (see Luke 4:18-19; Isa. 61:1-2).

Isaiah's words described the attributes of the Messiah's ministry and how the Messiah would lead, empowered by the Holy Spirit. The main focus of this ministry would be on the proclamation of good news to various kinds of people in need—the poor, the captives, the blind, and the oppressed. At one level, this ministry focuses on the spiritual needs of the people—captive to sin, blind to the good news, oppressed by evil, and spiritually bankrupt. At the same time, Isaiah had in mind the economic and material needs of the people. The ministry of the Messiah would answer both eternal and temporal needs, both spiritual and physical needs.

For this reason, the church proclaims the work of Jesus for the salvation of the world while simultaneously working alongside others in bringing physical and temporal relief to suffering. James 1:27 tells us, "Pure and undefiled religion before God the Father is this: to look after orphans and widows in their distress and to keep oneself unstained from the world."

Jesus redeemed us from spiritual captivity. How does His redemption lead us to meet physical and temporal needs of people around us?

Why is it problematic for Christians to focus only on spiritual problems and fail to meet physical needs?

Jesus boldly declared that right there, before the eyes of the people in the synagogue, Isaiah's prophecy had been fulfilled in Him. The people were taken aback by the claim. They were amazed at His eloquence, but they couldn't believe that a carpenter's son could be so special.

So, the people in Jesus' hometown did what many do today with Jesus. Unwilling to accept His claims, they reject His uniqueness. They shrink Him down to the rest of humanity. They discredit Jesus by making Him seem less valuable than He is.

What are some ways people try to discredit the uniqueness of Jesus?

Why is it important that Christians highlight the fact that Jesus is distinct from others?

2 Jesus Faced Rejection

After Jesus read from the scroll of Isaiah, He saw the unbelief in the hearts of the people and began to anticipate their rejection of Him, just as God's people had often rejected the prophets.

> 23 Then he said to them, "No doubt you will quote this proverb to me: 'Doctor, heal yourself. What we've heard that took place in Capernaum, do here in your hometown also.'"
>
> 24 He also said, "Truly I tell you, no prophet is accepted in his hometown. 25 But I say to you, there were certainly many widows in Israel in Elijah's days, when the sky was shut up for three years and six months while a great famine came over all the land. 26 Yet Elijah was not sent to any of them except a widow at Zarephath in Sidon. 27 And in the prophet Elisha's time, there were many in Israel who had leprosy, and yet not one of them was cleansed except Naaman the Syrian."
>
> LUKE 4:23-27

You may have heard this statement before, a phrase that originated with Jesus: "No prophet is accepted in his hometown." The idea is similar to another common phrase today: "Familiarity breeds contempt." The people in Jesus' hometown did not see Him as special or unique; they saw Him as ordinary. What's more, they didn't care for His message, even though they would have liked to see His miracles.

Sometimes it's difficult to notice the growth of people who are closest to us. You know what it's like. You don't see the day-to-day growth of your siblings or children, but you notice immediately how they or their children have changed when you visit friends or family you haven't seen in a while. Distance gives us perspective on people.

In a similar way, the people in Nazareth saw Jesus grow up before their eyes. But they could not reconcile the presence of this prophet who was before them with the young boy who had grown up in their midst. They would not accept the truth of Jesus' words as He read the scroll of Isaiah.

What do you think about Jesus' decision not to perform miracles in Nazareth?

Why did Jesus respond to their rejection in this way?

In the previous section, we saw that Jesus shocked His hearers in two ways: First, He claimed to be the fulfillment of Isaiah's prophecy. The second way was by proclaiming the grace of God and the day of freedom. That second shock included Jesus' words regarding recipients of miracles outside of God's people.

The day of freedom Jesus proclaimed was not just for the Jewish people. God was doing something that would include other nations, just as He promised Abraham to bless all the nations of the earth through Abraham (see Gen. 12:3).

To make this point, Jesus confronted the unbelief of the people in Nazareth by referring them to two Old Testament stories, one with Elijah (see 1 Kings 17:1-24) and one with Elisha (see 2 Kings 5:1-19). Both of these men were mighty prophets of God. In both accounts, God did something miraculous for people who were not part of the official "people of God"; rather, they were Gentiles.

The telling of these two stories took on new meaning in Jesus' time. He was putting Himself in the line of prophets who had been raised up by God. Jesus was putting the people of Nazareth in the line of ancient Israelites who had rejected the prophets of old. No wonder they were offended at His message! In hearing this word from Jesus, their hearts grew harder.

When have you faced rejection because of your faith?

3 Jesus Continued His Ministry

The people of Nazareth reacted first with amazement and then with anger. Read how they responded to Jesus' message:

> 28 When they heard this, everyone in the synagogue was enraged.
> 29 They got up, drove him out of town, and brought him to the edge of the hill that their town was built on, intending to hurl him over the cliff. 30 But he passed right through the crowd and went on his way.
>
> LUKE 4:28-30

The people were so enraged at Jesus' words that they wanted to throw Him off a cliff so that He would fall to His death. Although Jesus' mission included His substitutionary death, this was not the appointed time for Him to die. We don't know exactly how Jesus passed through the crowd and avoided death in this moment. Some commentators think Jesus' escape was miraculous. Others believe He simply managed to get away. Either way, it is clear that the situation in Nazareth was dire.

Jesus was rejected by His own people, just as Isaiah predicted 700 years before (see Isa. 53:3). Despite the rejection from the people in His own hometown, Jesus pressed on to fulfill the ministry God called Him to.

> In what ways have you seen the work of God continue in spite of opposition and obstacles?

The rejection of Jesus goes back to the sinfulness of the human heart. John 3:19 reminds us: "This is the judgment: The light has come into the world, and people loved darkness rather than the light because their deeds were evil." As people rejected Jesus in His day, sadly they still reject Him in ours. People react harshly to the truth of the gospel because it exposes the darkness of our hearts.

Jesus warned those who followed Him that they would endure the same rejection He did (see Matt. 5:10-12; John 15:19-23). We are to take comfort in these moments because Jesus modeled for us what it looks like to encounter rejection, endure it, and triumph over it. The Holy Spirit gives us the strength to press on through the seasons of rejection.

Second Corinthians 4:1-12 encourages us to remain active in the ministry God has called us to—primarily making the gospel of Jesus Christ known. We will face many pressures, but they will never crush us. We will become tired, but never will we die of exhaustion. Our comfort flows from understanding that God the Holy Spirit empowers us.

Our value as believers who seek to live on mission is found not in numbers or metrics. Rather, it is found in God the Holy Spirit, who indwells us and with whom we walk in step while stewarding the gospel message.

Faithfulness to Christ looks like this:

- Abiding in constant fellowship with God (see John 15:1-11);

- Allowing God's Word to be the umpire for all of our actions (see Col. 3:15-17);

- Submitting to the Holy Spirit's control by allowing Him to influence our attitudes, action, and speech (see Eph. 5:18) so He can bear fruit through us (see Gal. 5:22-23) while surfacing in times of prayer the sinfulness in our hearts that we are in need of confessing (see 1 John 1:8-10).

As we do these things, we will endure persecution and suffering, but we will rejoice to be counted as one of God's people who faced rejection, just like Jesus. This is the tangible expression of God the Holy Spirit's ministry through our lives, benefiting those inside the body.

In what ways does our endurance in the midst of rejection or opposition strengthen our witness and mission?

GROUP STUDY

Warm Up

As a group, read 2 Corinthians 1:3-7.

> ³ Praise the God and Father of our Lord Jesus Christ, the Father of mercies and the God of all comfort. ⁴ He comforts us in all our affliction, so that we may be able to comfort those who are in any kind of affliction, through the comfort we ourselves receive from God. ⁵ For as the sufferings of Christ overflow to us, so through Christ our comfort also overflows. ⁶ If we are afflicted, it is for your comfort and salvation. If we are comforted, it is for your comfort, which is experienced in your endurance of the same sufferings that we suffer. ⁷ And our hope for you is firm, because we know that as you share in the sufferings, so you will share in the comfort.
>
> 2 CORINTHIANS 1:3-7

In times of rejection, we remember the words of the apostle Paul in 2 Corinthians 1:3-7. As God has comforted us during times of suffering and affliction, we now are able to come alongside and comfort other believers who are suffering through various afflictions.

What encouraging words would you offer to a young believer facing rejection because of a stand for Jesus?

How can our group/church support and strengthen Christians across the world who face rejection and persecution for the sake of Christ?

"Try and work your home life or business life according to the rule of Jesus Christ and you will find ... a continual semi-cultured sneering ridicule; nothing can stand that but absolute devotion to Jesus Christ ... Christianity is other-worldliness in the midst of this-worldliness."[2]

OSWALD CHAMBERS

Discussion

1. Jesus redeemed us from spiritual captivity. How does His redemption lead us to meet physical and temporal needs of people around us?

2. Why is it problematic for Christians to focus only on spiritual problems and fail to meet physical needs?

3. What are some ways people try to discredit the uniqueness of Jesus?

4. Why is it important that Christians highlight the fact that Jesus is distinct from others?

5. What do you think about Jesus' decision not to perform miracles in Nazareth? Why did Jesus respond to their rejection in this way?

6. When have you faced rejection because of your faith?

7. In what ways have you seen the work of God continue in spite of opposition and obstacles?

8. In what ways does our endurance in the midst of rejection or opposition strengthen our witness and mission?

Conclusion

What a Savior we have in Jesus! Although He faced rejection and opposition, the ministry of the Holy Spirit empowered Him to remain steady in order to complete the mission to seek and save those who were lost. It's comforting to know that God had not abandoned Israel and that hundreds of years before Jesus was even born, God spoke to the prophet Isaiah to share a message that freedom from sin was coming.

We can find the hope we need to endure when we face rejection and persecution. It does not matter if it comes from a stranger we just met, a coworker we have been sharing the gospel with, or even a family member who rejects us for our stance for Jesus. We can rally among other believers and be encouraged and reminded of how Jesus endured opposition for our sake! May we reengage with those who have rejected us with the refreshing truths of the gospel of Jesus who is seeking to ransom them from captivity!

Spend some time praying this for you and for your group:

"God, thank You that Jesus is the fulfillment of Your promise to redeem people out of the captivity of sin. Remind us that we can always depend on Your power to endure when we are faced with rejection and persecution. And help us to press forward with our witness and mission in spite of it."

1. Paul John Isaak, "John," in *Africa Bible Commentary*, ed. Tokunboh Adeyemo (Grand Rapids: Zondervan, 2010) [eBook].
2. Oswald Chambers, in *The Quotable Oswald Chambers*, comp. and ed. David McCasland (Grand Rapids: Oswald Chambers Publications Associations, 2008), 191.
3. C.S. Lewis, *Mere Christianity* (New York: HarperOne, 1980), 52.

"You must make your choice. Either this man was, and is, the Son of God: or else a madman or something worse. You can shut him up for a fool, you can spit at him and kill him as a demon; or you can fall at his feet and call him Lord and God. But let us not come with any patronising nonsense about his being a great human teacher. He has not left that open to us. He did not intend to." [3]

C.S. LEWIS

NOTES

SESSION 6

JESUS AND ZACCHAEUS

"Zacchaeus' story is an incredible picture of gospel-motivated generosity. In Zacchaeus, we see a stingy, fiscally corrupt man become one of the most generous people in the entire Bible." [1]

J.D. GREEAR

INDIVIDUAL STUDY

The story of Zacchaeus is memorable because it is about a man of small stature who was so eager to see Jesus that he climbed into a tree to catch a glimpse of Him. When I read about the effort Zacchaeus put forth to see Jesus, I think back to a guy that our family used to pick up and take to our church service every week. Going out of our way to pick him up meant we had to leave for Sunday services earlier than usual, and our weekly routine began to frustrate me.

One Sunday morning, I complained about the inconvenience of picking up this young man. Why couldn't he just take the bus? My mother sat me down and told me the man's story—one that included a history of abuse and parental neglect. He had recently come to Christ, and although various people offered to take him to church, the man lived far enough away that it was difficult to maintain consistent transportation. The man was so eager to worship that he began walking—more than four hours—to church and back, rising before the sun to get a head start.

Needless to say, I stopped complaining about having to get up a little earlier to pick up this man for church! Instead of looking down on him, I was convicted by the effort and sacrifice he had made to worship with believers in Christ. The conversation with my mom quickly shifted. Consequently, I was recommending that we buy him breakfast on the way.

What sacrifices have you have seen people make in order to worship Jesus?

What stands out about their choices?

In this session, we read about Zacchaeus, a man whose example shows us what overflowing gratitude looks like in the heart of a sinner who encounters the love of Jesus. Zacchaeus overcame obstacles to see Jesus, obeyed Jesus' command, and welcomed Jesus into his home. Zacchaeus then showed incredible generosity as a result of his transformation. Understanding Jesus' desire to seek and save the lost, we see ourselves in the story of Zacchaeus and are called to walk in repentance and to give generously to advance the gospel.

Zacchaeus Overcame Obstacles

The story of Zacchaeus is recorded in Luke 19, as Jesus entered Jericho on His way to Jerusalem. Take a look:

> [1] He entered Jericho and was passing through. [2] There was a man named Zacchaeus who was a chief tax collector, and he was rich. [3] He was trying to see who Jesus was, but he was not able because of the crowd, since he was a short man. [4] So running ahead, he climbed up a sycamore tree to see Jesus, since he was about to pass that way.
>
> LUKE 19:1-4

Did you notice how Luke described Zacchaeus? He mentioned two facts: Zacchaeus was a chief tax collector, and he was rich. Tax collectors in Jesus' day were despised by the Jewish people. Why? Because tax collectors were Jews, too, but they collaborated with the Roman officials who oppressed God's people. What's more, it was common practice for Jewish tax collectors to extort money above the Roman tax, and then they would use the extra money to pad their pockets and live in luxury.

Consider this analogy: If you've ever traveled, you are probably familiar with tollbooths. Every few miles or so, you go through a tollbooth and pay a fee so you can remain on that stretch of highway. Imagine if you knew the toll was $3, but the collector asked for $10. Wouldn't you be frustrated? You'd want to report the collector to the government officials.

In Jesus' day, the tax collectors were overcharging, but the people had no recourse—no one to turn to in order to report these practices. Furthermore, the people could see how these tax collectors were living. Like the description says, "He was rich"—rich because he had stolen from his fellow countrymen! Here we have a man who would have been viewed as a traitor—a man whose wealth was earned by sin and oppression. What an unlikely man to become a follower of Jesus!

What are some other stories in the Gospels where Jesus interacted with wealthy people or taught about riches?

What do we learn from these stories?

What's interesting about Zacchaeus is that he actually wanted to see Jesus. The only problem was that he was short. Perhaps the people who hated tax collectors purposefully blocked Zacchaeus so that he wouldn't be able to get through, maybe as a way of getting back at him for his extortion. Whatever the case, Zacchaeus was determined to see Jesus, and so he climbed up into a tree.

Why was Zacchaeus so determined? Was he familiar with Matthew—one of Jesus' followers who had once been a tax collector, too? Did Zacchaeus wonder if perhaps Jesus would embrace him the way He had Matthew? The text doesn't say, but it is likely that word had gotten out about Jesus' willingness to associate with tax collectors and other types of sinners. Maybe Zacchaeus was hoping that he would be transformed by Jesus' teaching.

The crowds got in the way of Zacchaeus seeing Jesus. In what ways can crowds (or even churches) get in the way of people seeing Jesus today?

Zacchaeus' decision to climb up into a tree was unheard of in that day. Men didn't climb trees. It was not "dignified" for a man with his clout to do such a thing. But Zacchaeus didn't care. He may have been short, and the crowd may have been in the way, but with a childlike enthusiasm, he did what he had to do. He positioned himself in a way that he could see Jesus.

What hinders us from exercising childlike faith in Jesus?

What does childlike faith look like in practice?

Jesus Ignored Opposition

The crowds made it hard for Zacchaeus to see Jesus, but Jesus looked over the heads of the crowd and saw Zacchaeus anyway. Read what happened next:

> [5] When Jesus came to the place, he looked up and said to him, "Zacchaeus, hurry and come down because today it is necessary for me to stay at your house."
>
> [6] So he quickly came down and welcomed him joyfully. [7] All who saw it began to complain, "He's gone to stay with a sinful man."
> LUKE 19:5-7

Jesus looked up and noticed Zacchaeus. He asked Zacchaeus to come down because He wanted to spend time at the man's house.

Notice who initiated this conversation: Jesus! And did you catch how Jesus called the man by his first name? It's a beautiful scene. Jesus took notice of this man, acknowledged him, called out his name (the name of a despised chief tax collector), and then expressed His desire to spend time in this traitor's home!

Not surprisingly, the people who saw this interaction were appalled. To be a guest in someone's home meant you were "in fellowship" with them. It was like having an outstretched arm of love and acceptance or giving a warm embrace. In the eyes of the onlookers, Jesus was spending time with one of the "bad guys"—someone who had done terrible and selfish things as part of his career. Why would a righteous teacher, someone who claimed to be the Messiah, want to spend time in fellowship with a man known for his wickedness?

What barriers do religious people sometimes put up that make it difficult to engage people who need Christ?

What are some categories of people we may be inclined to think of as "unreachable" by God's grace?

The people began to complain: "He's gone to stay with a sinful man." Here we see the people in the crowd assuming Zacchaeus was beyond redemption, and so they were puzzled why Jesus wanted to spend time with such a person. They had written off any possibility that God would or could accept him.

Before we condemn the crowds, we ought to put ourselves in their situation. What about us? What about the times we hold a grudge because of other people's sinful actions against us, and because of the hurt they may have caused us, we write them off as if God cannot reach them? Or what about people who pursue addictions, engage in sinful exploits, or express hostility or rage toward Christians? Do we consider them beyond redemption?

Meanwhile, stories like this one show us a Savior who pursues all kinds of sinners. Is that not our testimony? We, too, were selfishly pursuing our own dreams at the expense of others while neglecting the grace of God, and yet, Jesus called us by name and welcomed us into His family.

There was a young man I grew up with; we were in school together for many years. After I met the Lord Jesus, I became unashamed in my witness for the gospel during my last years in high school. It shocked my friend, even to the point that my constant witnessing to him in class frustrated him. My heart was grieved, because I knew that he understood where I was coming from, but his rejection of Jesus broke my heart.

There came a time when I stopped being vocal about the gospel and focused my ministry on prayers of intercession. When I began to see that his heart was still hard toward the things of God, I gave up. I thought that he was never going to embrace Jesus, and from that day forward, I just assumed he would stay lost.

A few years later, my friend sent me an email. While living in another city, he'd gone through a few moments of crisis, and God had sent a Christian into his life to share the good news of Jesus. He told me he was convinced that during all of our dialogue, God was sowing gospel seeds into his heart. I wept when I read that email because I recall the very day that I thought he was unredeemable. His email convicted me to recognize that I should never doubt the power of God.

What is the significance of Jesus ignoring His opposition in order to spend time with Zacchaeus?

3 Jesus Celebrates Repentance

Zacchaeus' response to Jesus involved conviction, confession, and repentance.

> 8 But Zacchaeus stood there and said to the Lord, "Look, I'll give half of my possessions to the poor, Lord. And if I have extorted anything from anyone, I'll pay back four times as much."
>
> 9 "Today salvation has come to this house," Jesus told him, "because he too is a son of Abraham. 10 For the Son of Man has come to seek and to save the lost."
> LUKE 19:8-10

Zacchaeus quickly came down from the tree to welcome Jesus, but then he stopped walking and just stood there. I wonder what was going through his mind. Hearing the crowd, perhaps it was the fact that he knew the crowd's complaint was right. He was guilty of extortion!

Immediately, without being prompted directly by anyone else, Zacchaeus told Jesus he would give half of his possessions to the poor. If he had exhorted anything from anyone, he would pay back four times as much as he took. Here we see how Zacchaeus was convicted of his wrongdoing—to the point he willingly confessed his extortion and demonstrated his repentance by vowing to make full restoration and more to those he had victimized.

Why do you think Zacchaeus thought it was imperative he pay back the people he extorted money from?

What does this decision express about his heart?

Jesus responded by saying that salvation had come to Zacchaeus' house. Jesus was speaking about the tax collector's salvation. This moment is extraordinary because Jesus saw this man as "a son of Abraham"—meaning he had a covenant connection to the forefathers of Israel.

But Jesus claimed the man's salvation was based on his response to Jesus, not his pedigree going back to Abraham. What's more, saving faith expresses itself in a changed life, which is exactly what we see in Zacchaeus.

As Rey De Armas writes: "Because we have been shown generosity by Christ, we understand what it means to have someone be spiritually generous to us in our state of poverty. Zacchaeus was relationally and spiritually poor. Jesus was generous to him, and because of His generosity, Zacchaeus was no longer lost but found … Using Zacchaeus as an example, we can see how stinginess is a sign that we do not know the grace of God. Grace is not fairness. Grace is not a karmic state that allows us to repay God for the wonderful acts that He has done for us. Grace is receiving something that we could never deserve." [2]

Luke closed the dialogue between Jesus and Zacchaeus by sharing the thesis statement of the Gospel of Luke: "For the Son of Man has come to seek and to save the lost" (19:10). Jesus, the great physician, sought to heal those who are spiritually sick, infected by the disease of sin. Psalm 103:3 reminds us, "He forgives all your iniquity; he heals all your diseases." It was Jesus' mission to be the fulfillment of all that Luke 4:14-22 expresses (see Session 5).

The mission of Jesus was defined by His pursuit of the unrighteous—people born into sin, slaves to sin, and separated from God. This describes all of us! The mission that Jesus sought to fulfill regularly afforded Him the opportunities to engage with the outcasts of society. It was often these who, although rejected by society, embraced God's only plan of redemption for humanity.

Read 2 Corinthians 7:9-11 and describe the qualities of biblical repentance.

In the encounter between Jesus and Zacchaeus, how did Zacchaeus demonstrate some of the qualities Paul listed in this passage?

GROUP STUDY

Warm Up

Who are the people in your life who need to see Jesus but feel unreachable?

We must treat every person we come in contact with or remain in contact with as someone who might embrace Jesus as Savior. God calls us to pursue people we may assume are beyond God's saving grace, to show them the way to salvation in Jesus. We may face opposition for building a friendship with lost people, but we can learn from the ministry model of Paul, who shared both the gospel and himself with the people he encountered (see 1 Thess. 2:8).

How are you helping others see Jesus? How might you be getting in the way?

How can you push past opposition in order to spend time with sinners who need Jesus?

"There is no crime in possessions, but there is crime in those who do not know how to use possessions. For the foolish, wealth is a temptation to vice, but for the wise, it is a help to virtue. Some receive an opportunity for salvation, but others acquire an obstacle of condemnation." [3]

MAXIMUS OF TURIN

Discussion

1. What are some other stories in the Gospels where Jesus interacted with wealthy people or taught about riches? What do we learn from these stories?

2. The crowds got in the way of Zacchaeus seeing Jesus. In what ways can crowds (or even churches) get in the way of people seeing Jesus today?

3. What hinders us from exercising childlike faith in Jesus?

4. What does childlike faith look like in practice?

5. What barriers do religious people sometimes put up that make it difficult to engage people who need Christ?

6. What is the significance of Jesus ignoring His opposition in order to spend time with Zacchaeus?

7. Why do you think Zacchaeus thought it was imperative he pay back the people he extorted money from? What does this decision express about his heart?

8. In the encounter between Jesus and Zacchaeus, how did Zacchaeus demonstrate some of the qualities Paul listed in 2 Corinthians 7:9-11?

Conclusion

God demonstrated His love by sending Jesus to seek and save the lost. While we were dead in our sins, Jesus came to die for us in our place (see Rom. 5:8). His substitutionary death, burial, and resurrection fulfilled His mission. God rejoices when sinners hear the gospel and are moved to admit their guilt, confess their sinfulness, and trust in the finished work of Jesus in order to be saved. Never should we believe that people are so far from God that they cannot be reached by His grace.

We who have embraced Jesus know this firsthand. And because of our encounter with Jesus, we can express our gratitude to our Savior by sharing His story with those we come in contact with and by sharing our resources with those in need.

Spend some time praying this for you and for your group:

> "God, thank You that none of us have gone so far that we are out of the reach of Your grace. Help us live with an awareness of the Zacchaeus-types who are around us. May we always be sensitive to Your Spirit as we seek to show people Christ."

1. J. D. Greear, "3 Critical Truths About Our Money," *JDGreear.com* [online], 4 December 2014 [cited 15 July 2016]. Available from the Internet: *www.jdgreear.com*.
2. Rey De Armas, "Do Not Steal," *The Gospel Project: Adult Leader Guide* (Summer 2014): 112-13.
3. Maximus of Turin, Sermons, 95-96, quoted in *Luke*, ed. Arthur A. Just Jr., vol. III in *Ancient Christian Commentary on Scripture: New Testament*, 291.
4. W. A. Criswell, "Zacchaeus Come Down," Criswell Sermon Library [online], 27 July 1969 [cited 15 July 2016]. Available from the Internet: *dev.wacriswell.com*.

"He knows his name ... How did the Lord know his name? He knows all of us. He knows your name. He knows where you live ... He knows your house and home ... And He knew of the hunger, and the spiritual thirst, and wanting in the heart of that little man up there atop that tree." [4]

W. A. CRISWELL

NOTES

SMALL-GROUP TIPS

Reading through this section and utilizing the suggested principles and practices will greatly enhance the group experience. First is to accept your limitations. You cannot transform a life. Your group must be devoted to the Bible, the Holy Spirit, and the power of Christian community. In doing so your group will have all the tools necessary to draw closer to God and to each other—and to experience heart transformation.

GENERAL TIPS:

- Prepare for each meeting by reviewing the material, praying for each group member, and asking the Holy Spirit to work through you as you point to Jesus each week.

- Make new attendees feel welcome.

- Think of ways to connect with group members away from group time. The amount of participation you have during your group meetings is directly related to the time you take to connect with your group members away from the group meeting. Consider sending emails, texts, or social networking messages encouraging members in their personal devotion times prior to the session.

MATERIALS NEEDED:

- Bible

- Bible study book

- Pen/pencil

PROVIDE RESOURCES FOR GUESTS:

- An inexpensive way to make first-time guests feel welcome is to provide them a copy of your Bible study book. Estimate how many first-time guests you can expect during the course of your study, and secure that number of books. What about people who have not yet visited your group? You can encourage them to visit by providing a copy of the Bible study book.